TO:

FROM:

theCouponCollection™

SOURCEBOOKS, INC.
NAPERVILLE, ILLINOIS

The Perfect

AQUARIUS
Coupons

A coupon gift to inspire
the best in you

SOURCEBOOKS, INC.®
NAPERVILLE, ILLINOIS

Published by Sourcebooks, Inc.
P.O. Box 4410, Naperville, Illinois 60567-4410
(630) 961-3900
FAX: (630) 961-2168
www.sourcebooks.com

ISBN 1-4022-0180-X

Printed and bound in the United States of America

AP   10 9 8 7 6 5 4 3 2 1

An Aquarian needs time alone for balance:
CANCEL ANY PLANS
and revel in your own company tonight.

Aquarians are warm
and caring, yet prize
their independence
and sometimes need
time alone.

theCouponCollection™

SOURCEBOOKS, INC.
NAPERVILLE, ILLINOIS

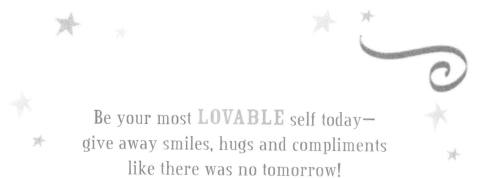

Be your most **LOVABLE** self today—
give away smiles, hugs and compliments
like there was no tomorrow!

Aquarians are
naturally friendly
and charming; they
sometimes seek
solitude, but they
return to the world
with renewed
enthusiasm for life.

Is your Aquarian idealism suffering?
Cheer yourself up by watching an
INSPIRING movie, like "Gandhi."

Beware the anger that comes from disillusionment. An Aquarian's high ideals are sometimes more than the world can live up to.

theCouponCollection™

SOURCEBOOKS, INC.®
NAPERVILLE, ILLINOIS

You have an **INTELLECTUAL CURIOSITY**
that just won't quit. Capitalize on it by signing up
for a new class or personal development seminar.

Both Aquarius and Pisces are usually extremely intelligent and inventive, drawn to the world of ideas.

theCoupon Collection™

SOURCEBOOKS, INC.
NAPERVILLE, ILLINOIS

NOTHING can hold down an Aquarian; go ahead and book that flight, plan that weekend, head for the hills!

Aquarius and
Sagittarius make a
great pair: both love
their freedom, and
understand when
others need it as well.

theCouponCollection™

SOURCEBOOKS, INC.®
NAPERVILLE, ILLINOIS

INDULGE YOUR LOVE OF BEAUTY;
go to lunch at an art gallery or museum.
Take an old friend; or meet a new one
and find out how much you have in common.

Is there a Libra in your future? Aquarius and Libra make ideal mates, sharing a love for beauty, society, and art.

theCouponCollection™

SOURCEBOOKS, INC.®
Naperville, Illinois

TREAT YOURSELF to a soothing footbath and take care of those delicate Aquarian ankles.

Each Zodiac sign is said to rule a particular part of the body—Aquarius rules the shins and ankles.

This coupon entitles you to **RELAX**
with a cup of steaming Earl Grey tea—
fragrant bergamot is good for the
insomnia that may trouble the Aquarian.

Aquarians' active minds sometimes interfere with their ability to relax and sleep peacefully.

theCouponCollection™

SOURCEBOOKS, INC.®
NAPERVILLE, ILLINOIS

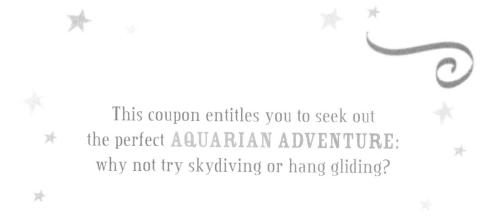

This coupon entitles you to seek out
the perfect **AQUARIAN ADVENTURE**:
why not try skydiving or hang gliding?

Both Gemini and Aquarius are Air signs—you appreciate plenty of clean, fresh air, and wide-open spaces.

theCouponCollection™

SOURCEBOOKS, INC.
Naperville, Illinois

Indulge your Aquarian tendency to **INNOVATE**—whip up a fabulous dessert out of whatever is on hand.

Aquarians love to
experiment; in fact,
you never quite stick
to the script, the
recipe—or the rules.

theCouponCollection™

SOURCEBOOKS, INC.®
NAPERVILLE, ILLINOIS

This coupon is good for a
browse-by-touch shopping expedition.
TREAT yourself to the softest, silkiest item
you can find and **SOOTHE** your Aquarian soul.

Aquarians tend to be fond of smooth, shiny fabrics, metals, and glass.

Need mental stimulation
for that active Aquarian mind?
TREAT YOURSELF to a trip to the
library or bookstore today.

Aquarians are the intellectuals of the Zodiac, exhibiting great independence of thought.

theCouponCollection™

SOURCEBOOKS, INC.
NAPERVILLE, ILLINOIS

You are known for your **ORIGINALITY**—
isn't it time for a more outrageous hairstyle?

Free-spirited Aquarius
is full of surprises,
making them lots of
fun to be around.

To get you centered, do some sit ups.
REMEMBER TO BREATHE!

Let an affectionate
Libra help you put
balance and harmony
in your life.

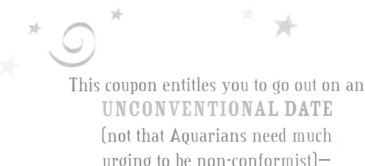

This coupon entitles you to go out on an
UNCONVENTIONAL DATE
(not that Aquarians need much
urging to be non-conformist)—
you pick the time, place, and event.

Aquarians find great enjoyment in love and romance, as long as they can maintain a certain amount of privacy and independence—a Cancer won't mind this a bit.

As an artist, you tend
to be **HIGHLY IMAGINATIVE**—
yield to your creative impulses and
buy a new set of paints,
chalk, or colored pencils.

Aquarius is recognized as among the most original and eccentric of the signs of the Zodiac.

theCouponCollection™

SOURCEBOOKS, INC.
NAPERVILLE, ILLINOIS

Investigate some second-hand stores—
search out an unusual glass ornament
or vase in a shade of blue that
SPEAKS TO YOUR SOUL.

A loving Taurus can
provide the security
and sensuous comfort
that Aquarius might
tend to miss out on.

theCouponCollection™

SOURCEBOOKS, INC.®
NAPERVILLE, ILLINOIS

SHOWER THE PEOPLE YOU LOVE
with your love and attention today—
make all those phone calls,
emails, and visits.

Sometimes those close
to a free-spirited
Aquarian need
reassurance that your
love of independence
doesn't mean you
don't care about them.

the**Coupon**Collection™

SOURCEBOOKS, INC.®
NAPERVILLE, ILLINOIS

To help your Aquarian **AIRINESS**
get a little grounded, try making something out of
clay or go and paint pottery. You'll probably
find this very soothing.

An earthy Virgo, who likes order, can provide the perfect balance for an airy Aquarius, who loves chaos, as long as they are tolerant of each others' differences.

YOUR ELEMENT IS AIR—
you'll never feel so free as when
you're walking outside on a windy day.
With this coupon, take some time off
and go get in your element.

An Aquarius who
hooks up with a Libra,
another Air sign, will
find a companion
who shares their love
of freedom.

theCouponCollection™

SOURCEBOOKS, INC.™
NAPERVILLE, ILLINOIS

WHILE AQUARIUS CAN BE EXPLOSIVE
when coming into contact with a Fire sign, try bringing
some of the warmth of the sun in, without the volatility.
On the next warm day, lie down in the
sun and soak up a few rays.

A fiery, energetic Aries and a spontaneous Aquarian together make for a red-hot romance.

theCouponCollection™

SOURCEBOOKS, INC.
NAPERVILLE, ILLINOIS

TO GROUND YOURSELF AFTER A LONG DAY,
go to the beach and dig your toes into the sand.

The natural common sense and down-to-earth quality of a Virgo may be just right for balancing a restless Aquarius.

theCouponCollection™

SOURCEBOOKS, INC.®
NAPERVILLE, ILLINOIS

YOU'RE EXPRESSIVE AND COMMUNICATIVE—
why not express yourself by singing at the top of your
lungs? This coupon entitles you to belt out one song of
your choice—either with the radio, alone in
the shower, or in front of friends.

When a happy-go-lucky Sagittarius teams up with an outrageous Aquarius, the results can be astonishing—just don't get arrested!

Some say that the sapphire
appeals most to the brilliant Aquarian.
Wear something today in
MAJESTIC SAPPHIRE BLUE—
chances are it's in your closet.

Aquarius and the
serious Capricorn will
balance each other
perfectly.

theCouponCollection™

SOURCEBOOKS, INC.™
NAPERVILLE, ILLINOIS

Aquarius is usually **POSITIVE** and **BRIGHT**
no matter what happens. The next time something
gets you down, use this coupon and do something
really fun to cheer yourself up.

Aquarius, find yourself an optimistic, freedom-loving Sagittarius, and you'll never stop having fun.

theCouponCollection™

SOURCEBOOKS, INC.
NAPERVILLE, ILLINOIS

Feeling volatile and unstable?
Try a seated yoga posture like "forward folding."
Sit with your legs extended, and reach for your toes.
BREATHE DEEPLY until you feel calm and centered.

A sensitive,
compassionate Cancer
can provide the
brilliant Aquarius
with a loving place to
come home to.

theCouponCollection™

SOURCEBOOKS, INC.®
NAPERVILLE, ILLINOIS

EXPRESS YOUR AQUARIAN SPIRIT—
wear a diaphanous scarf or shawl.

The esoteric, dreamy Pisces paired with the daring Aquarius will find no end of imaginative, creative fun.

theCouponCollection™

SOURCEBOOKS, INC.®
NAPERVILLE, ILLINOIS

With this coupon, INDULGE YOURSELF
on a hot-air balloon ride.
You'll be right in your element!

An adventurous,
passionate Aries
would love to sail off
into the wild blue
yonder with an airy
Aquarius.

theCouponCollection™

SOURCEBOOKS, INC.®
NAPERVILLE, ILLINOIS

Bring a little fire into your
AIRY EXISTENCE—
try wearing red, yellow, and orange.

The strong, warm-hearted Fire sign Leo with the sunny disposition is fascinated and challenged by the bold Aquarius.

the**Coupon**Collection™

SOURCEBOOKS, INC.®
NAPERVILLE, ILLINOIS

Aquarius is usually **HIGHLY MOTIVATED**.
Today's the day to get that new idea of
yours implemented. Go grab a couple of
cronies at work and get the ball rolling.

Hard-working,
meticulous Virgo is
the one that Aquarius
needs to help give
those brilliant dreams
some solid reality.

theCouponCollection™

SOURCEBOOKS, INC.®
NAPERVILLE ILLINOIS

FOR A FEW MINUTES OF AQUARIUS PEACE,
lie on the ground and gaze up at the clouds.

When two high-flying Aquarians get together, there's no end to the flow of ideas and creativity.

theCouponCollection™

SOURCEBOOKS, INC.
NAPERVILLE, ILLINOIS

It will always make an Aquarius **HAPPY** to hear the wind in the trees. Put up a wind chime and enjoy the beautiful sounds on a windy day.

A free-spirited
Aquarius can help an
intense, introverted
Scorpio to open up,
while the Scorpio's
dark sensuality can
bring emotional depth
to the life of the cool
Aquarius.

theCouponCollection™

SOURCEBOOKS, INC.®
NAPERVILLE, ILLINOIS

You feel best in a
SPACIOUS ENVIRONMENT—
get rid of the clutter in your home
and you'll be a happy Aquarius.

A gentle Virgo will be
sure to keep the
Aquarian's home
environment in
perfect order.

theCouponCollection™

SOURCEBOOKS, INC.
NAPERVILLE, ILLINOIS

THE PERFECT AQUARIUS
Born January 20 - February 18

Welcome to the world of the perfect Aquarius. Astrology is a powerful symbolic language for describing and interpreting human life and events on the Earth. This coupon book is a fun way to dip into that ancient pool of knowledge and make the most of the potential that lies in your nature.

WHY ASTROLOGY?

Astrologers believe that the makeup, configuration, and movement of the planets and stars correspond with events anywhere in the universe, including human lives, and that studying these cycles can help people understand the past and present, and even predict the future. By mapping the position of the other planets in our galaxy, the moon, and the sun in the heavens when you were born, astrology finds indications of the circumstances you may encounter, as well as clues to your basic personality traits and how you relate to others.

THE TWELVE HOUSES

Imagine a wheel in space that circles the Earth like a cigar band. This band is divided into twelve sections, or houses, because the sun spends approximately one month in each area in relationship to the Earth, as our planet makes its yearly journey around the sun. (In ancient times, of course, it was believed that the sun was, in fact, circling the Earth.) The wheel of the Zodiac divides the heavens into the twelve traditional astrological groupings, each of which is assigned certain polarities, qualities, and elements. The Zodiac wheel also makes clear the relationships among the signs. For instance, Aquarius is located on the wheel directly opposite the sign of Leo, and is in many ways the Lion's opposite in values and interests.

Although your sun sign provides the basic key to your personality, in astrology, *each* of the planets in our galaxy, as well as the moon, has influences which are expressed in your life.

THE TWO POLARITIES

All the signs are divided into two polarities, either masculine or feminine types. The male signs are more active and extroverted, as in the Chinese philosophical term yang, which refers to the positive, bright, and masculine. The female signs are considered more sensitive, meditative, and inward looking, as in the Chinese yin, which is the negative, dark, and feminine. Of course, astrology has always acknowledged that everyone embodies both female and male energies in their nature.

As an Aquarian, your essence is masculine. You have strong male traits in your essential nature, which will interact with all the cultural and societal influences you encounter, as well as the other influences in your astrological chart (for instance, the location of the moon at your birth).

THE THREE QUALITIES

A lesser known aspect of astrology divides the signs into three types of qualities—cardinal, fixed, or mutable—which have to do with how you relate to the world. The four cardinal signs (Aries, Cancer, Libra, and Capricorn) are the most assertive, the most interested in making changes, leading and being in control. The four mutable signs (Gemini, Virgo, Sagittarius, and Pisces) are the most changeable and open to outside influences.

As an Aquarius, you are one of the four fixed signs, along with Taurus, Leo, and Scorpio. You are less concerned with outside influences—in fact, you probably tend to resist them. The good news is, you can be strong, consistent, and stable. The bad news is, you may find it difficult to change a fixed mindset or let in positive influences.

THE FOUR ELEMENTS

Each sign of the Zodiac is also associated with one of the four elements: fire, earth, air, or water, which lend certain

symbol of Aquarius is the Water Bearer, which leads many
e mistaken assumption that Aquarius is a water sign. You,
rius, are one of the air signs of the Zodiac, along with
ni and Libra. The air signs are the thinkers, the
lectuals, and the planners. You are all about ideas, thought,
communication. Aquarius, in particular, has a great ability
ur out new ideas.

YOUR RULING PLANETS

rding to ancient astrology, the sun and moon ruled one house
and the five other known planets (Mercury, Venus, Mars,
er, and Saturn) ruled two houses each. As they were

characteristics to those signs. The three fire signs ar[e]
and Sagittarius—they tend to be energetic, impatien[t]
and...well, fiery.

The three earth signs are Taurus, Virgo, and Capri[corn]
earthy types are—you guessed it—down to earth. The[y]
practical, reliable, and cautious.

The emotional water signs are Cancer, Scorpio, and [Pisces]
are the sensitive ones, the dreamers, the spiritualist[s]
capable of great depths of emotion and compassion.

The[
to t[
Aqu[
Gem[
inte[
and [
to p[

Acc[
each[
Jupi[

discovered, the farther distant planets of Uranus, Neptune, and Pluto were added to the ancient system, resulting in some houses having a "secondary" ruler.

You, Aquarius, are one of those with a co-ruler. The ancient ruling planet of the house of Aquarius is Saturn, and the "modern" co-ruler is Uranus. This makes you one of the most interesting and mysterious signs, considering that these two planets are completely contradictory in nature!

The Saturn side of your nature is authoritarian, while the Uranian side is eccentric, chaotic, radical, and rebellious. In other words, you insist on personal freedom and unconventional ideas, and you may find yourself imposing your unusual ways on others!

Remember that Aquarius is a masculine—positive, outgoing—sign, and you are much concerned with society and humanitarian ideals. Just remember, too, that, Aquarius is a fixed sign, and you may want to check and see if the opinions about which you are being so stubborn could use some updating.

MIXING WITH THE OTHER ELEMENTS
With your contradictory nature, you can use the support of the Earth signs (Taurus, Virgo, and Capricorn) for stability. These

friends, while they may be relatively lacking in imagination, will keep you grounded. They can help give your brilliant flow of ideas a solid, practical form.

Be careful around your Fire sign friends (Aries, Leo, and Sagittarius)—all your combined energy could be explosive. There's no lack of power, ambition, or enthusiasm here; if you stay on track and keep from burning out, together you can change the world.

The combination of Air and Water yields some beautiful possibilities. Around people of the Water signs (Cancer, Scorpio, and Pisces), Aquarians can express the poetry and beauty in their natures. The dreamy imaginations and sensitivity of the Water signs can elevate your intelligence and talent for innovation to new heights. Just keep some Fire and Earth signs around if you want to occasionally come down out of the clouds.

WHAT'S YOUR MOON?

The position of the moon at your birth exerts a strong influence on the basic elements of your Aquarius personality. The house occupied by the Moon channels the expression of your personality in such areas as maternal qualities, domestic interests, and emotional needs.

For example, a moon in Aries brings fire to your cool, intellectual Aquarius nature: as a parent, your Aquarius loyalty, originality, and good communication skills will be complemented by Aries enthusiasm and warmth, making you a lively and successful parent. In love, a moon in Aries makes you the most passionate of the Aquarians (who tend to be somewhat detached in one-on-one relationships). You may want to investigate how your sun sign is tempered by the other influences in your astrological chart—it's both entertaining and a rich source of imagery and meaning.

AQUARIUS IN LOVE

In general, Aquarians tend to be friendly and humanitarian, but can be rather distant in their personal relationships. Your freedom is important to you, and you may hesitate to commit until you feel secure in your ability to maintain a certain level of independence. Your intelligence and creativity make you a fascinating companion, while your stubbornness and unpredictably can drive your partner crazy. At your best, you are loving, honest, loyal, and sincere. You might want to watch out for people who bring out your possible tendencies to be cool and unemotional, contrary and intractable, or outlandish and chaotic.

Take a look at the coupons in this book: they are designed to help you explore your compatibility with other signs, bring out your best traits, and help you with your worst. Have a great time exploring the wisdom of the stars!

theCouponCollection™

SOURCEBOOKS, INC.®
NAPERVILLE, ILLINOIS

INDULGE YOUR FRIENDLY NATURE:
Stock up at the deli on your way home from work,
and invite some friends for an impromptu party.

When an outgoing Aquarius teams up with a sociable Sagittarius, chances are good you'll enjoy the company of lots of friends.

You're known for being
INVENTIVE and **UNPREDICTABLE**:
Go ahead, make someone's day with an
unexpected message, gift, or plan.

Free-spirited
Aquarians are full of
surprises, making
them lots of fun to be
around.

theCouponCollection™

SOURCEBOOKS, INC.
NAPERVILLE, ILLINOIS